# LONG LIVE
## THE *Preacher*

**Prayers & Decrees for Preachers**

# Ryan LeStrange

# TABLE OF CONTENTS

# DECREES & PRAYERS
### FOR *Preachers*

For there is no distinction between Jew and Greek; for the same *Lord* is Lord of all, abounding in riches for all who call on Him; for "Whoever will call on the name of the Lord will be saved."

How then will they call on Him in whom they have not believed? How will they believe in Him whom they have not heard? And how will they hear without a preacher?

—Romans 10:12-14

Through the glorious Gospel of Jesus Christ, every person alive has access to salvation, redemption, and new life. There is no sin too big and no stain too dark to block the grace that Jesus has made available to humanity. This promise is not to some, but to all. To all who will hear, believe, and receive, the Gospel of redemption and life in the Spirit is available.

1

> According to the glorious gospel of the blessed God which was committed to my trust.
>
> —1 Timothy 1:11 (NKJV)

Timothy was a steward of the glorious Gospel. Today, the Gospel is entrusted to the Church and heralded through the lips of preachers everywhere in every corner of society. Preachers have the unique opportunity and responsibility to declare the power, redemption, and love of Jesus. From generation to generation, the Gospel has been carried upon the shoulders of daring men and women who believed God and released His Word.

This is the burden of a preacher. They feel something that Jeremiah described like fire shut up in their bones.

> Then I said, "I will not make mention of Him,
> Nor speak anymore in His name."
> But *His word* was in my heart like a burning fire
> Shut up in my bones;
> I was weary of holding *it* back,
> And I could not."
>
> —Jeremiah 20:9 (NKJV)

The Word of the Lord beckons preachers to speak His glorious Gospel in times of struggle and in times of great success, when it seems easy and when it seems like a great battle. Preachers must remain consistent. They must remain committed.

The nations will not hear without the preachers. In each generation, God takes His purifying power and releases it to preachers. He tasks them with the awesome responsibility of stewarding the life-changing words of Jesus. Romans 10:14 says, "How will they hear without a preacher?" This is not a mere question, but a fearful decree. Generations hang in the balance waiting upon the daring, waiting upon the committed, waiting upon the willing. Today, at the reading of these words, God is taking his Holy Scroll and touching the lips of yet another generation who will go to the ends of the earth for Him and release His Word.

> And he said unto them, Go ye into all the world, and preach the gospel to every creature.
>
> —Mark 16:15 (KJV)

This is why the enemy hates preachers. Those who have been branded by fire and redeemed of the Lord pose a great threat to the kingdom of darkness. The enemy works against preachers through attacks, mental warfare, accusations, calamity, discouragement, and fear. He takes everything that he has and slings it at those called of God to release the mystery and power of the Gospel. The warfare has a mission. That mission is to silence the proclamation of the Word of God. The devil hates the lips of a preacher for they are weapons of mass destruction. He does all that he can to defeat and bombard the preacher.

Prayer is a great opposing force against the works of hell. It establishes our hearts in the purposes of God. It pushes back against the lies of hell. It dispatches angelic backup. It creates strength in our inner-man to rise and meet the need. This book is designed for two purposes:

1. **To give every preacher some scripture and prayer guides.**

   The world needs you! Our generation needs you. The future needs you. Your labor is not in vain. You are an instrument of the Kingdom of God. You are anointed, appointed, and destined for great things.

2. **To give the people of God tools to use to intercede for preachers everywhere.**

   You may not see it, but they are under immense pressure. Hell is bombarding every area of their lives. Your prayers are powerful. Take these prayers and stand with preachers. You are standing for and with the proclaiming of Jesus Christ unto the ends of the earth.

The world needs strong, fiery, bold preachers. God is not finished saving people, delivering them, and filling them with the Holy Spirit. There is a great work to do. There is a mandate for the end. There is a harvest to win! Every preacher's cry is: "Here am I, Lord; send me." The cry of every intercessor is: "Lord, we will pray for the preachers."

Each of us is a part of God's global army. The time is now! We must go. Let's pray together! Let's bind the powers of hell! Let's fight the good fight! Let's go to the ends of the earth with the fire and glory of God! Let's go with the strong love of Jesus and the glorious power of His Spirit! Let's go with tenacity and daring obedience! Let's go with prayers and power! Let's go and preach this Gospel. God, send the preachers!

> "The gospel is preached in the ears of all men; it only comes with power to some. The power that is in the gospel does not lie in the eloquence of the preacher otherwise men would be converters of souls. Nor does it lie in the preacher's learning; otherwise it could consist of the wisdom of men. We might preach till our tongues rotted, till we should exhaust our lungs and die, but never a soul would be converted unless there were mysterious power going with it—the Holy Ghost changing the will of man. O Sirs! We might as well preach to stone walls as preach to humanity unless the Holy Ghost be with the word, to give it power to convert the soul."
>
> **—Charles Spurgeon**

"The backslider likes the preaching that wouldn't hit the side of a house, while the real disciple is delighted when the truth brings him to his knees."

**—Billy Sunday**

"To preach Christ is to feed the soul, to justify it, to set it free, and to save it, if it believes the preaching."

**—Martin Luther (*On Christian Liberty*)**

"Give me 100 preachers who fear nothing but sin and desire nothing but God; such alone will shake the gates of hell."

**—John Wesley**

# PEACE

> Casting all your care upon him; for he careth for you.
>
> —1 Peter 5:7 (KJV)

Lord, today I cast every care concerning my life and ministry upon you. I decree that I walk in total peace and surrender. I cast down every thought that leads my mind to worry. I choose to think on good things. I decree that your power is working in my mind. I command every spirit of fear and anxiety to leave me now, in the name of Jesus. I declare that my mind is alert and rested. I declare that my body is stress-free. I refuse to worry and stress. Thank you, Lord, for supernatural peace overwhelming every area of my life, in Jesus' name. Amen.

## UTTERANCE

> And for me, that utterance may be given to me, that I may open my mouth boldly to make known the mystery of the gospel...
>
> —Ephesian 6:19 (NKJV)

Lord, I don't want to preach messages that are void of your power and revelation. I pray that when I open my mouth, divine utterances would come forth. I decree that my tongue would be as the pen of a ready writer. I stir up the gift of preaching in my belly, in the name of Jesus! I command revelation to break forth. I command the rivers of God to burst forth. I command the scrolls to be unfolded. I decree that I speak as your oracle, Lord. Do not let me deviate from the assignment that you have for me every time I minister, in the name of Jesus. Amen.

## RIGHT PEOPLE

Lord, I thank you for the right people in my life and ministry. I decree that the right people are coming and the wrong people are leaving. I bind and break the spirit of depression and isolation off of my life concerning the exit of people. I declare that I serve you first, Lord. I decree that I am focused on your mandate for my life. I walk in love with people, but I trust you above every man. I am not moved by the departure of people. I call forth the right people in every area of my ministry, in the name of Jesus. Amen.

## RIGHT TIMING

> He hath made every thing beautiful in his time:
> also he hath set the world in their heart, so that
> no man can find out the work that God maketh
> from the beginning to the end.
>
> —Ecclesiastes 3:11 (KJV)

Lord, I thank you that I am in sync with your timing for my life. I decree that my ministry stays in tune with divine timing. I break and bind every spirit that would push me outside of your timing. I declare that I am patient and that I properly discern times and seasons in my life. I am not stuck in an expired season. I hear the current word of the Lord for my life and ministry! I am not afraid of divine change. I do not move outside of your rhythm. I move by the speed of the Holy Ghost! I say that my steps are ordered of you and I operate in heaven's timing for my life, in Jesus' name. Amen.

## FAMILY

> A devout man and one who feared God with
> all his household, and gave many alms to the
> Jewish people and prayed to God continually.
>
> —Acts 10:2

Lord, I thank you that my family belongs to you. I thank you that your plans prevail for us. I bind every foul spirit that would try to attack us. I release the power of the blood of Jesus over my family. I commission angels to protect my family. I pray that the pressures of ministry do not overtake us. I claim that my family is born again and on fire for you according to Acts 16:31. No weapon that is formed against my family prospers. I thank you that my family is supernaturally shielded from lies and attacks. I thank you that we are growing in wisdom, favor, and grace. I thank you that your purposes are fulfilled in my family, in the name of Jesus. Amen.

## HEALTH

> And He Himself bore our sins in His body on the cross, so that we might die to sin and live to righteousness; for by His wounds you were healed.
>
> —1 Peter 2:24

Thank you, Lord, that I am healed by the stripes of Jesus. I rebuke sickness and disease. I decree that the stress of ministry will not adversely affect my physical body. I thank you that the Spirit of God lives in me and quickens my mortal body. I release healing into every cell, every fiber, every system, and every organ in my body. I decree that God's healing power is flowing through me, aborting the plans of the enemy. I decree that I am strong and not weak. I will live and not die, and declare the works of the Lord. I will be satisfied with long life. Healing is in my covenant with you, Lord. I thank you for divine healing in my body, in Jesus' name. Amen.

## SOUL PROSPERITY

Beloved, I pray that in all respects you may prosper and be in good health, just as your soul prospers.

—3 John 2:2

Father, I thank you that I prosper in my soul. I decree that I properly identify your mandate for my life, and that I fully live it. I am not distracted, nor am I unduly influenced by the thoughts, opinions, and attitudes of others. I have found my calling, I have embraced my personality, and I am complete in you. I decree that I love my purpose and the plan you have tailor-made for me. I decree that my soul excels as I live out your will for my life. I know that I am fearfully and wonderfully made with a unique purpose and a personality to match my assignment. I embrace who you made me to be, and live in the midst of your plan for me, in the name of Jesus. Amen.

## SPIRIT LEADING

For as many as are led by the Spirit of God, these are sons of God.

—Romans 8:14 (NKJV)

Thank you, Lord, that I am led by your Spirit. I decree that I clearly hear and see the plan and purpose for my life and ministry. I come against demonic traps and snares. I decree that the discerning of spirits is in operation in my life and ministry. Lord, reveal your will and plan to me. Reveal the right timing and also, the people in my life. Speak to me in the night season and the early morning. Drop revelation in my spirit. Send people across my path to confirm what you are saying. I decree that I will not miss your will for my life. I have ears to hear and eyes to see what you are saying to me, in Jesus' name. Amen.

## FRIENDSHIP WITH GOD

Walk with the wise and become wise, for a companion of fools suffers harm.

—Proverbs 13:20 (NIV)

Greater love has no one than this: to lay down one's life for one's friends.

—John 15:13 (NIV)

As iron sharpens iron, so one person sharpens another.

—Proverbs 27:17 (NIV)

Lord, I thank you for a close and intimate relationship with you. I decree that I walk with you and prioritize nearness to you. I am not distracted or consumed in an unhealthy way with ministry. I thank you, Lord, for helping me to remain a seeker of your glory and presence. I bind and break all distractions off my life, in Jesus' name. I decree that I do not operate under a condemning spirit. I decree that I walk in your presence and hear from you on a consistent basis. Thank you, Father, for your deep love and affection for me, in Jesus' name. Amen.

## KINGDOM ASSIGNMENTS

> For we are his workmanship, created in Christ Jesus unto good works, which God hath before ordained that we should walk in them.
>
> —Ephesians 2:10 (KJV)

Lord, I thank you for your assignments in my life and ministry. I decree that I know where to be, when to be there, and who to be with. I decree that your Spirit is leading and guiding my every step. Thank you, Father, for clarity of purpose and calling. Thank you, Father, for supernatural confirmation of every dream and vision that you have given to me. I confess that I will not be overwhelmed by the vast nature of your calling on my life. I call forth partners in destiny in my life and ministry, in the name of Jesus. I say that my steps are ordered of you, and I boldly navigate your will for my life, in the name of Jesus. Amen.

## NO DEPRESSION

> For who hath known the mind of the Lord, that he may instruct him? But we have the mind of Christ.
>
> —1 Corinthians 2:16 (KJV)

I decree that I have the mind of Christ, in the name of Jesus. I bind and cast out every spirit of depression, heaviness, and slumber, in the name of Jesus. I thank you, Lord, that you have not given to me the spirit of fear or anxiety. You have given me a sound mind. I decree that my thought patterns are clear. I decree that I think on good things. I let go of every pain and wound, and I ask for your healing power to flow into my mind, will, and emotions, in the name of Jesus. Amen.

## NO FEAR

> There is no fear in love; but perfect love casteth out fear: because fear hath torment. He that feareth is not made perfect in love.
>
> —1 John 4:18 (KJV)

I cast out the spirit of fear, in the name of Jesus! Fear, go from me now. I thank you, Lord, that your perfect love overwhelms every part of my life. I know that you love me and that your love paid the price for every sin in my life. I decree that I am supernaturally led and charged by your spirit. I have supernatural might, strength, and ability, in the name of Jesus. I am not afraid. I walk by faith and not by sight, in Jesus' name. Amen.

## NO ANXIETY

Be anxious for nothing, but in everything by prayer and supplication with thanksgiving let your requests be made known to God. And the peace of God, which surpasses all comprehension, will guard your hearts and your minds in Christ Jesus.

Finally, brethren, whatever is true, whatever is honorable, whatever is right, whatever is pure, whatever is lovely, whatever is of good repute, if there is any excellence and if anything worthy of praise, dwell on these things.

—Philippians 4:6-8

Thank you, Lord, that I am free from anxiety. I choose not to give place to the enemy. I decree that my mind is fixed upon you. I cast down every thought that is contrary to your will in my life and ministry. I cast the spirit of fear, torment, and anxiety out, in the name of Jesus. I command these spirits to go. I release the peace of God that passes all understanding over my life. I decree supernatural peace over my mind. I command my mind to be at rest, in the name of Jesus. I release stress, anxiety, and torment, in the name of Jesus. Amen.

## NO STRESS

> Peace I leave with you; My peace I give to you;
> not as the world gives do I give to you. Do not let
> your heart be troubled, nor let it be fearful.
>
> —John 14:27

I receive the peace of God in every area of my life. I
decree that I am not stressed out. I break stress off my
life, in the name of Jesus. I command every thought
of worry and tension to go from me now. I speak the
supernatural and abiding peace of God to over-
whelm my soul now, in the name of Jesus. Thank you,
Lord, that I walk in peace. Thank you, Lord, that my
assignment is covered in peace. You are the Prince of
Peace, and I live surrendered to you; therefore, I am
blanketed in your peace, in the name of Jesus. Amen.

## NO DEMONIC BACKLASH

> Be of sober *spirit*, be on the alert. Your adversary,
> the devil, prowls around like a roaring lion,
> seeking someone to devour. But resist him, firm
> in *your* faith, knowing that the same experiences
> of suffering are being accomplished by your
> brethren who are in the world.
>
> —1 Peter 5:8-9

Thank you, Lord, that I am not moved by the lies of the
enemy about me, to me, or against my assignment.

I bind up and render harmless all retaliatory attacks of the enemy against my ministry. I loose the blood of Jesus over my mind, my body, my ministry, and my family. I am protected and covered by the blood of Jesus. I break all spiritual backlash, in the name of Jesus. I decree that no weapon formed against me prospers. Thank you, Lord, that I see and hear clearly. Thank you, Lord, that I am submitted to your plans and purpose. Thank you, Lord, that I am sober-minded and set apart for your plans. I am neither confused nor discouraged. I am stable and steadfast. I am fixed upon your Word and established in your plans. I decree that I am immovable. I decree that I endure and overcome the powers, in Jesus' name. Amen.

## LANDS & BUILDINGS

Then it shall come about when the Lord your God brings you into the land which He swore to your fathers, Abraham, Isaac and Jacob, to give you, great and splendid cities which you did not build, and houses full of all good things which you did not fill, and hewn cisterns which you did not dig, vineyards and olive trees which you did not plant, and you eat and are satisfied...

—Deuteronomy 6:10-11

Thank you, Lord, for the land, buildings, and resources that have been appointed for my life and my assignment. I decree that I have all that I need to fulfill your will in my life and ministry. I decree abundance. I decree ownership. I am the head and not the tail. I am above and not beneath. Thank you for supernatural increase and abundance in my life, in the name of Jesus. Amen.

## HARVEST OF SOULS

> Ask of Me, and I will give *You*
> The nations *for* Your inheritance,
> And the ends of the earth *for* Your possession.
>
> —Psalm 2:8 (NKJV)

Thank you, Lord, for souls coming into the Kingdom of God. I decree that people are being saved through the ministry you have given to me, in the name of Jesus. Thank you that the harvest is plentiful and you have created me to be an instrument of harvest in the earth. I pray even now that the power of the Gospel is going forth preparing the hearts of men and women for salvation. Lord grant unto me boldness to declare the Gospel to the lost and hurting in this hour. Give me favor with men and women who need to know your saving grace, in the name of Jesus. Amen.

## HARVEST OF FINANCES

> But this *I say*: He who sows sparingly will also reap sparingly, and he who sows bountifully will also reap bountifully. *So let* each one *give* as he purposes in his heart, not grudgingly or of necessity; for God loves a cheerful giver. And God *is* able to make all grace abound towards you, that you, always having all sufficiency in all *things*, may have an abundance for every good work.
>
> —2 Corinthians 9:6-8 (NKJV)

Thank you, Lord, that I am a sower. I choose to sow bountifully and therefore, I expect to reap bountifully. I decree financial harvest in my life and ministry. I decree abundant harvest. I say that resources are coming to me now. I say that promotion is coming to me now. I decree benefactors, underwriters, and supernatural seeds coming to my ministry now. You are the Lord of the harvest, and I thank you for divine financial harvest in my life. I walk in your blessings. Everything I need is supplied, and I have more than enough resources. I walk in abundance and prosperity. I have more than enough. I am blessed to be a blessing, in the name of Jesus. Amen.

## HARVEST OF HEALING

And He said, "If you will give earnest heed to the voice of the Lord your God, and do what is right in His sight, and give ear to His commandments, and keep all His statutes, I will put none of the diseases on you which I have put on the Egyptians; for I, the Lord, am your healer."

—Exodus 15:26

Thank you, Lord, for miracles, signs, and wonders in my life and ministry. You are the God who heals. I decree a harvest of the miraculous in my life and ministry. I believe in your healing power. I stir up the gift of faith. I stir up the working of miracles. I stir up the gifts of healings. Thank you, Lord, for unusual healing miracles in my life. I expect your healing power to flow in my life and my ministry. I place a demand upon you now for divine healing, in the name of Jesus. Amen.

## HARVEST OF REVELATION

But the Helper (Comforter, Advocate, Intercessor—Counselor, Strengthener, Standby), the Holy Spirit, whom the Father will send in My name [in My place, to represent Me and act on My behalf], He will teach you all things. And He will help you remember everything that I have told you.

—John 14:26 (AMP)

Thank you, Lord, for a harvest of revelation in my life and ministry. Thank you, Lord, for your active power in my life. Thank you, Holy Spirit, for teaching me, leading me, and guiding me into all truth. Thank you for supernatural insight and understanding of your word. I decree that the spirit of wisdom and revelation is active in my life. I decree that I have supernatural genius. I decree that my understanding is supernatural. I receive the mysteries of God in my life. I receive insight. I receive wisdom. I walk in the spirit of counsel and might. I walk in the wisdom of God, in the name of Jesus. Amen.

# PRAYERS FOR *Freedom*

## FREEDOM FROM PRIDE

> Therefore I, the prisoner of the Lord, implore you to walk in a manner worthy of the calling with which you have been called, with all humility and gentleness, with patience, showing tolerance for one another in love...
>
> —Ephesians 4:1-2

Thank you, Lord, for humility in my life. Oh, God, I ask you to create in me a clean heart and renew a right spirit within me. Lord, help me to stay focused on you and on your nature in my life. I resist pride and break every prideful spirit off of my life. I cast out the spirit of pride and Leviathan. I thank you, Lord, that I am fully surrendered to you and obedient to your plans in my life. I decree that I live surrendered to you. I decree that I am quick to repent. Lord, I thank you for your leadership in my life. I decree that I am fully surrendered to you in my words, in my thoughts, and in my actions, in the name of Jesus. Amen.

## FREEDOM FROM CONDEMNATION

> Therefore there is now no condemnation for those who are in Christ Jesus.
>
> —Romans 8:1

Thank you, Lord, that I am free from every condemning spirit. I decree your love in my life. I decree that I am planted in you, in your heart, in your mind, and in your ways. Your blood has set me free from accusation and bondage. By the blood, I am made free. By the blood, I am made brand new. By the blood of Jesus, I am redeemed. I do not look back at my past. I do not live in past mistakes or struggles. I live in Christ Jesus. I am saved, healed, redeemed, and set free through the blood of Jesus. Amen.

## FREEDOM FROM INADEQUACY

> The steps of a man are established by the Lord,
> And He delights in his way.
> When he falls, he will not be hurled headlong,
> Because the Lord is the One who holds his hand.
>
> —Psalms 37:23-24

Thank you, Lord, that you are more than enough! I refuse to embrace feelings of inadequacy. I will not partner with any condemning spirit. I know that you are leading and guiding me. I tap into the spirit of might upon my life. I tap into the dunamis power of your Spirit. I am well able through your blood! I am well able through the power of your cross. I am well able through the power of your resurrection. The blood of Jesus is more than enough for me. Thank you, Lord, for your provision in every area. I decree that I am strong in you. I decree that I am brave in you. I decree that I am mighty in you, in the name of Jesus. Amen.

## FREEDOM FROM THE FEAR OF MAN

The fear of man brings a snare,
But he who trusts in the Lord will be exalted.

—Proverbs 29:25

Thank you, Father, that I am free from the fear of man. I decree that I walk in radical obedience to you. When you speak, I listen. When you lead, I follow. When you reveal your will for my life and ministry, I embrace it. Thank you, Lord, for total deliverance from the fear of man. I decree that I obey you and walk in your will for my life and ministry, in the name of Jesus. Amen.

## FREEDOM FROM WORD CURSES

Then the Lord spoke to Moses, saying, "Speak to Aaron and to his sons, saying, 'Thus you shall bless the sons of Israel. You shall say to them:

The Lord bless you, and keep you;
The Lord make His face shine on you,
And be gracious to you;
The Lord lift up His countenance on you,
And give you peace.'"

—Numbers 6:22-26

Lord, I thank you that I am blessed and not cursed! I am the head and not the tail. I renounce and break every word curse that has been spoken over me, in the name of Jesus. I command demonic utterances to fall to the ground. I rend every word curse null and void by the power of the blood of Jesus. I thank you, Lord, that I am blessed, that you are keeping me, and that you are causing your face to shine upon me. You give me perfect peace. I decree your blessing over my mind, my home, my body, my family, and everything that concerns me, in the name of Jesus Christ of Nazareth. Amen.

# PRAYERS FOR Anointing

## ANOINTING

> And it shall come to pass in that day, that his burden shall be taken away from off thy shoulder, and his yoke from off thy neck, and the yoke shall be destroyed because of the anointing.
>
> —Isaiah 10:27 (KJV)

Father, I thank you for your anointing. It is your super on my natural. I decree that I walk in the anointing. I walk in my purpose. I walk in my assignment. Your supernatural power and miracle-working ability is with me everywhere I go, in the name of Jesus. Every facet of my life is divinely charged and filled with your anointing. I am anointed because the Anointed One lives in me. I am supernaturally equipped and able. Your life and resurrection power is in me and working through me. I decree unusual measures of anointing flowing in my life and ministry. I decree the anointing to set captives free, destroy yokes, and accomplish unusual exploits, in the mighty name of Jesus. Amen.

## ANOINTING OF POWER

> How God anointed Jesus of Nazareth with the Holy Ghost and with power: who went about doing good, and healing all that were oppressed of the devil; for God was with him.
>
> —Acts 10:38 (KJV)

Lord, I thank you for your anointing and power on my life and ministry. I thank you for uncommon miracles! I thank you for your life-changing, yoke-destroying anointing and power working in me and through me. I decree that rivers of living water flow from my belly. I stir up rivers of joy, rivers of healing, rivers of salvation, and rivers of deliverance and declare that they flow from my innermost being. I decree that your power is working now. Your power is working as I move in the call upon my life. Your power is working in the lives of all those I meet. My mouth is filled with your words. My hands are filled with your power. My belly is filled with your rivers. The sick are healed, the bound are set free, and lives are changed because of your anointing. I yield and surrender to your power. I expect your power to show up when I preach. I expect your power to show up when I pray. I expect your power to show up when I minister. Thank you, Lord, for your anointing and power in my life and in everything I am doing in your Kingdom, in the name of Jesus. Amen.

## ANOINTING OF BREAKTHROUGH (BREAKER ANOINTING)

> "The breaker is come up before them: they have broken up, and have passed through the gate, and are gone out by it: and their king shall pass before them, and the Lord on the head of them."

> —Micah 2:13 (KJV)

I decree the breaker anointing in my life, in the name of Jesus. Release the power of breakthrough! Thank you, Lord, for the breaker supernaturally propelling me beyond my own abilities. Thank you for the breaking down of every demonic wall and blockade. I command mental blockades to be broken down. I command family blockades to be broken down. I command regional blockades to be broken down. I command financial blockades to be broken down. I command spirits of infirmity to go, in the name of Jesus. I decree that every barrier and blockade that is affecting my physical body must fall and crumble under the power of the breaker anointing. I release the power of the breaker in every area of my life and ministry, in the name of Jesus. My ministry is not limited. I walk in breakthrough. God's power is upon me and my ministry to break through, in Jesus's name. Amen.

# PRAYERS FOR THE Spirit

## SPIRITUAL STAMINA

For this reason also, since the day we heard *of it*, we have not ceased to pray for you and to ask that you may be filled with the knowledge of His will in all spiritual wisdom and understanding, so that you will walk in a manner worthy of the Lord, to please *Him* in all respects, bearing fruit in every good work and increasing in the knowledge of God; strengthened with all power, according to His glorious might, or the attaining of all steadfastness and patience; joyously giving thanks to the Father, who has qualified us to share in the inheritance of the saints in Light.

—Colossians 1:9-12

Thank you, Lord, for spiritual stamina. I decree that I am strengthened by your power. I decree that the spirit of life is working in me and through me now. I decree that I endure and conquer all attacks of the enemy. I release your might over my life and ministry. I declare the spirit of might is active in my life, in the name of Jesus. I release your resurrection power over my ministry. My ministry is filled with your life and strength. I confess that I am strong and not weak. I am filled with joy and strength by your Spirit. Thank you, Lord, for the victory. I do not quit! I do not believe the lies of the devil. I do not give in to defeat. I boldly stand upon the Word of God with faith that does not waiver, in the name of Jesus. Amen.

## SPIRITUAL WISDOM

For the Lord gives wisdom;
From His mouth *come* knowledge and
understanding.
He stores up sound wisdom for the upright;
*He is* a shield to those who walk in integrity

—Proverbs 2:6-7

Thank you, Lord, for your wisdom in my life. I decree that I walk in your wisdom. I make wise plans by heeding your voice. I am wise in my decisions. I am wise in my conversations. I am wise in my thinking. Thank you, Lord, that you have given me wisdom to lead and wisdom to minister to your people. I decree your mind in my life. I do not walk according to my own plans or ideas. I walk according to your will. You are leading and guiding every step. You are releasing supernatural understanding and revelation in my life. Thank you, Lord, that I grow in your wisdom, in Jesus' name. Amen.

# PRAYERS FOR *Wisdom*

## WISE FRIENDS

> He that walketh with wise men shall be wise: but a companion of fools shall be destroyed.
>
> —Proverbs 13:20 (KJV)

Father, I thank you for wise friends in my life. I thank you for friends that help me see your plan and purpose for my life. I thank you for friends who stir up your call and plan for my life. I thank you for spiritually strong, stable friends. I thank you for emotionally healthy friends. I thank you for reliable friends. I decree that you are bringing the right friends to my life, in the name of Jesus. I decree that I walk in wisdom in all of my relationships. I decree your wisdom and leading in my relationships, in the name of Jesus. Amen.

## WISE WORDS

The Lord God has given Me
The tongue of the learned,
That I should know how to speak
A word in season to *him who is* weary.
He awakens Me morning by morning,
He awakens My ear
To hear as the learned.

—Isaiah 50:4 (NKJV)

Thank you, Lord, that I speak with the tongue of the learned. I decree that my words are led by your Spirit. You said that the power of life and death is in my tongue. Thank you, Lord, that I release blessings and not curses from my mouth, in the name of Jesus. I know that my tongue is prophetic, and I am called to speak according to your Word, not my emotions. Lord, I ask you to continually remind me of the responsibility that I have to speak in agreement with your plans for my life. I decree that my tongue is prophetic and that I speak according to your mind and promises, not according to my own mind or understanding, in Jesus' name. Amen.

## WISE DIRECTION & PLANS

For which one of you, when he wants to build a tower, does not first sit down and calculate the cost to see if he has enough to complete it?

Otherwise, when he has laid a foundation and is not able to finish, all who observe it begin to ridicule him...

—Luke 14:28-29

Lord, I thank you that I am a strategic planner and thinker. I decree that I move in a wise direction for my life and ministry. My steps are ordered of you. My calling is ordained by you. I declare your wisdom in my strategy and decisions. I break and bind the spirit of rebellion off my life. I decree that I am fully submitted to your plans and purposes. I decree that I move in sync with your heart and plans for my life. I refuse to make unwise decisions. Thank you, Lord, for wise building, planning, and dreaming. I decree that my mind lines up with your mind, and my vision lines up with your vision, and my ways line up with your ways, in the name of Jesus. Amen.

# PRAYERS FOR *Exposure*

## EXPOSURE OF DEMONIC PLOTS

> "For nothing is hidden that will not become evident, nor *anything* secret that will not be known and come to light."
>
> —Luke 8:17

I decree the exposure of all hidden demonic plots against me, my ministry, and my family. I decree that the undercover schemes against my life, my ministry, my assignment, my family, and my finances are exposed. I decree the light of God shines brightly upon my life and reveals the secret operations of the kingdom of darkness against me. I decree divine exposure and supernatural protection. No plot against my mind prospers. No plot against my family or relationships prospers. No plot against my finances prospers. No plot against my calling or assignment prospers. I speak a release of God's power and protection. I bind and break all demonic plots against me and release God's strength, wisdom, and strategies to overcome, in the name of Jesus. Amen.

## EXPOSURE OF HIDDEN DEMONS

> No wonder, for even Satan disguises himself as an angel of light.
>
> —2 Corinthians 11:14

Thank you, Lord, for the gift of the discerning of spirits in operation in my life and ministry. I decree that hidden devils are revealed, in the name of Jesus. My spiritual senses are alert. I see and know in the realm of the spirit. I am not deceived. I am not confused. I am not overcome by demonic entities, in the name of Jesus. Lord, I thank you for sobriety and clarity in my life and assignment, in the name of Jesus. Let every hidden spirit be revealed. Shine your light on my ministry and my life. Quicken my spirit, and alert me to hidden spirits and assignments, in the name of Jesus. Amen.

## EXPOSURE OF FALSE MOTIVES

> "For nothing is hidden, except to be revealed; nor has *anything* been secret, but that it would come to light."
>
> —Mark 4:22

Thank, you, Lord for divine insight concerning the motives of people in my life. I decree that wisdom and Spirit-leading are in operation in my life to reveal demonic agendas and enticements. I decree that I am led by your Spirit and that your wisdom is operating in my life. You supernaturally reveal false motives that are sent to hinder and impede your call upon my life, in the name of Jesus. I am not misled or falsely directed. I decree that I rightly discern flattery and exaggeration. I decree that I discern all lies and deceptive conversations. I decree that your protection is upon my life, my assignment, and my family. You protect me from wrong connections, plans, and agendas, in the name of Jesus. Amen.

# PRAYERS
## FOR THE
*Right Decisions*

## RIGHT TEAM

> Behold, how good and how pleasant it is for brethren to dwell together in unity!
>
> It is like the precious ointment upon the head, that ran down upon the beard, even Aaron's beard: that went down to the skirts of his garments;
>
> As the dew of Hermon, and as the dew that descended upon the mountains of Zion: for there the Lord commanded the blessing, even life for evermore.
>
> —Psalm 133:1-3 (KJV)

Thank, you, Lord for the right team in my life and ministry. I decree that you are sending me the right people and removing the wrong ones. I decree supernatural wisdom concerning the team that is appointed for my assignment. Thank you, Lord, that my team moves in unity. I decree that Psalms 133 is working in our midst. There is unity and a release of fresh oil. I thank you, Lord, for your provision and leadership concerning team members. I decree that I am a wise leader, and that I move in sync with you, in the name of Jesus. Amen.

## RIGHT LEADERSHIP

> Remember those who led you, who spoke the word of God to you; and considering the result of their conduct, imitate their faith.
>
> —Hebrews 13:7

Lord, I thank you for the right leaders in my life and ministry. Thank you that I have rightly discerned those that you have appointed to speak into my life. Thank you for the gifts that they are to me. Help me to always be a blessing to other leaders, to sow into them, and to show my appreciation. I decree that I am honorable toward my leadership, and therefore, there is a flow of blessing upon my life and ministry. I decree that I am wise in my relationships and connections. I decree that I walk in wisdom and integrity toward my leaders. I decree that I am a blessing to my leadership and not a burden. I decree that I add to their lives, and pray for them faithfully, in the name of Jesus. Amen.

# ADDITIONAL
## *Prayers*

## OPEN DOORS

> "A man's gift makes room for him
> And brings him before great men."

> —Proverbs 18:16

Father, I decree that the right doors open for my ministry and the wrong doors slam shut. I thank you for doors of opportunity. I thank you for favorable doors. I decree that doors of influence open. I decree doors of the supernatural open. I decree that doors into regions and territories open. I decree the opening of economic doors. I bind every spirit of distraction that would attempt to lead me through the wrong doors. I thank you, Lord, for the opening of divine doors and the blockage of all deceptive doors. You said that my gift would make room for me, and I am standing upon that promise. I decree that the gift you have placed in me brings me to the right places at the right time, in the mighty name of Jesus. Amen.

## FIRST LOVE

> But seek first His kingdom and His righteousness, and all these things will be added to you.
>
> —Matthew 6:33

Lord, I thank you that I seek you first. I decree that I am continually seeking after you, your heart, and your ways. I bind and break all distractions and confusion off my life. I refuse to be distracted. I refuse to move in the wrong direction. I thank you that before you ever gave me a ministry to people, you called me to love you and be loved by you. I thank you that the spirit of worship is strong in me, and that I pursue your presence without shame or fear of man. I decree that I am in pursuit of you in every area of my life, in the name of Jesus. Amen.

## FAITHFULNESS TO ASSIGNMENT

> I thank Christ Jesus our Lord, who has strengthened me, because He considered me faithful, putting me into service...
>
> —1 Timothy 1:12

Lord, I count you faithful! You never let me down. All of your promises concerning me and my calling are yes and amen. I decree that I am faithful to the mandate upon my life. As you have been so faithful and kind to me, so am I also committed to pursue and fulfill your assignment for me. I decree that I am strong and steadfast. I decree that I am not moved by the lies and attacks of the enemy concerning my calling. I decree that I am delivered from the fear of man. I decree that I am fruitful and abounding in every good work. I decree that I am focused and steadfast. I am immovable in the work of the Lord. I am in pursuit of your best, and nothing less. Thank you, Lord, for your faithfulness in my life, and thank you for your strength and stability in my life. I declare that I will fully administrate and execute my calling, in the name of Jesus. Amen.

## BREAK CONFUSION

"Trust in the Lord with all your heart
And do not lean on your own understanding."

—Proverbs 3:5

Lord, I break and bind all confusion. I command my mind to be clear and my thought patterns to be normal. Every spirit of confusion has to go from me now, in the name of Jesus! I am resolute and focused. I know my mandate and plan. I know the direction that I am to go, and I gladly follow God and His plan for my life. I thank you, Lord, for clarity and vision in my life. I thank you for focus and accuracy in my assignment. I decree that I am moving with you in the wisdom of your spirit, in the name of Jesus. Amen.

## RESOURCES

> And God is able to make all grace abound to you, so that always having all sufficiency in everything, you may have an abundance for every good deed...
>
> —2 Corinthians 9:8

Father, I thank you for your provision in my life and ministry. I decree that everything I need has already been provided for me. I decree that lands and buildings are mine, in the name of Jesus. I decree that money is coming to me to do your will on the earth. I call forth seeds, harvests, and miraculous supplies of wealth and increase. I am not bound by natural economic laws, but move in the anointing for wealth and abundance. I walk in supernatural provision, in the name of Jesus. I thank you, Lord, that you have already provided the right people to fulfill all that you have called me to do. I prophesy the right people in the right places in my ministry, in the name of Jesus. Lord, I trust you in every area as my provider, in Jesus' name. Amen.

# KINGDOM
*Preachers*

There is no greater responsibility than to herald the glorious Gospel of Jesus Christ. It is a sovereign calling to share the story of Jesus and His redemption of humanity. We have been both called and appointed for this divine task.

> After these things the Lord appointed other seventy also, and sent them two and two before his face into every city and place, whither he himself would come.
>
> —Luke 10:1 (KJV)

Jesus sent seventy of His disciples out to share the good news. He commissioned them to go forth two by two. There were thirty-five teams of Kingdom preachers loosed in the territory, armed with the power and authority of the Kingdom of God. These preachers were not tasked with the preaching of a tepid message that would pacify the hearts of the religious. They were charged to go forth and heal the sick, cast out demons, and announce the reality of the Kingdom of God in the earth. They were sent as ambassadors of a greater Kingdom than those of this earth.

In much the same way, God's preachers are being sent today into a drifting society. We are being tasked with sounding the alarm and proclaiming the reality of heaven and hell. We are called to stand between the living and the dead pleading for the souls of mankind. Preaching is not a popular art. It should be the cry of surrendered men and women who have seen the Lord, and had the painful and fearful experience of their lips being touched with the fiery coal that Isaiah witnessed!

> In the year of King Uzziah's death I saw the Lord sitting on a throne, lofty and exalted, with the train of His robe filling the temple. Seraphim stood above Him, each having six wings: with two he covered his face, and with two he covered his feet, and with two he flew. And one called out to another and said,
>
> > "Holy, Holy, Holy, is the Lord of hosts,
> > The whole earth is full of His glory."
>
> And the foundations of the thresholds trembled at the voice of him who called out, while the temple was filling with smoke. Then I said,

"Woe is me, for I am ruined!
Because I am a man of unclean lips,
And I live among a people of unclean lips;
For my eyes have seen the King, the Lord of
hosts."

Then one of the seraphim flew to me with a
burning coal in his hand, which he had taken
from the altar with tongs. He touched my mouth
*with it* and said, "Behold, this has touched your
lips; and your iniquity is taken away and your sin
is forgiven."

Then I heard the voice of the Lord, saying, "Whom
shall I send, and who will go for Us?" Then I said,
"Here am I. Send me!"

—Isaiah 6:1-8

During the encounter of the prophet Isaiah, God
asked a simple question; "Whom shall I send?" I feel
this is the same question that is being asked now in
this generation. Who will go? Who will boldly and
unashamedly proclaim the Gospel? Who will lay
hands on the sick? Who will rip down the demonic
pythons gripping regions and people? Who will be
audacious enough to believe God for the healing
of incurable diseases? Who will challenge dry
and dead atmospheres? Who will announce the
sovereign Lord? Who will make the people ready for
the Lord? Who will teach, preach, declare, expound,

and demonstrate? Who will shepherd, guide, build, compel, win, reveal, establish, explain, love, lead, and pour into the people? Who will build the next great wave of churches? Who will carry the apostolic banner to nations and regions? Who will go as God's prophet to a dying world? Who will tap into the mysteries of God and teach the Church? Who will win the lost? Who will love and care for the flock of God?

Who is ready to lose their life to find His? Who is ready to carry the weight of this glorious Gospel? Who is ready to stand before the weary hearts and pour out the water of his Word? I believe God is looking for our "yes"! He is looking for us to say what Isaiah said: "Here am I Lord, send me!" These are the words of the preacher. The preacher goes in spite of their flaws. The preacher goes in spite of the sacrifice. The preacher goes in spite of their insecurities. The preacher is not sent without fire! The angel is taking the coal and touching your lips. The Lord is filling your mouth with His words! All he needs from you is your "yes."

I am the Lord your God, Who brought you up out of the land of Egypt. Open your mouth wide and I will fill it.

But My people would not hearken to My voice, and Israel would have none of Me.

So I gave them up to their own hearts' lust *and* let them go after their own stubborn will, that they might follow their own counsels.

Oh, that My people would listen to Me, that Israel would walk in My ways!

Speedily then I would subdue their enemies and turn My hand against their adversaries.

[Had Israel listened to Me in Egypt, then] those who hated the Lord would have come cringing before Him, and their defeat would have lasted forever.

[God] would feed [Israel now] also with the finest of the wheat; and with honey out of the rock would I satisfy you.

—Psalms 81:10-16 (AMPC)

Open your mouth wide and I will fill it! That was the word of the Lord to His people. You open your mouth wide when you are hungry. The prophetic picture here is simple: when you are hungry, you will be filled. A preacher is one who is feasting on the revelation and majesty of the Lord. The preacher is like an artist who catches a glimpse of the reality of the beautiful Jesus, and then attempts to convey the view (revelation) of His majesty to the people through the art of words and the anointing of the Holy Spirit. The preacher is recalling what he or she has seen in the secret place.

The preacher builds their arsenal in two ways. First, great preaching is birthed in pursuit. Powerless are the words of a preacher who does not pray! A preacher is in constant pursuit and meditation through various avenues of prayer and reflection. A sermon, a teaching, or an insight could come at any moment. A preacher will quickly grab a napkin at lunch to scribble a passing nugget of insight before they lose it. The preacher does not live disconnected. The truly life-changing messages are borne of the Spirit in the place of pursuit and prayer.

The second place where great preaching is birthed is in study. A preacher is reading the Bible and allowing the Bible to read them! A preacher has a life-giving textbook. They are in continual search of the mind of God. They are examining the Scriptures in a repetitious manner, trying to gain another glimpse of Jesus buried somewhere in the sacred text. The preacher understands that the mind of God is released in the word of God.

> All Scripture is inspired by God and profitable for teaching, for reproof, for correction, for training in righteousness; so that the man of God may be adequate, equipped for every good work.
>
> —2 Timothy 3:16-17

Scripture has been inspired by God. It is the building block of transformation. The preacher must be a student of the Word of God. They must be famished for nourishment that only comes from Scripture. The preacher must love and value the Bible. They must find the answers to the deep questions of life, society, climate, culture, and shifting times in God's eternal Word. The preacher must not rest in man's wisdom or understanding, but must represent a more authentic realm of truth. The preacher must communicate the Scriptures with relevance, grace, and authority because they have been unveiled in times of private study and pursuit.

The preacher is not a casual reader of the Word of God, but a student of the mind and revelation of God. The preacher is one who diligently and continually dives deep into the Word of God. The preacher cannot wait to find time to study God's Word.

To the preacher, everything is a message! Life is a sermon. The preacher finds inspiration in everything around them. They constantly see parables and poetic communication in the daily affairs of life. Just as life is a song to the minstrel, so is a sermon to the preacher. The preacher is born to preach. The preacher does not preach to live, but lives to preach. The preacher will try to hang it up in times of heartache and frustration, but the itch will return. The void will remain. For it is the preacher that is born for a time and a people. It is the preacher that is unveiled as God's instrument of communication. It is the preacher that is God's warning system to a dying world. It is the preacher that is sent, appointed, and anointed for this time.

Preaching may be challenging. Preaching may be frustrating. Preaching may push you far beyond your comfort zone, but it is through the "foolishness" of preaching that God reaches a broken heart and brings it into the Kingdom. It is the art of preaching that releases new wine to a dry people. It is the rhythm of preaching that resets the lives of the broken. Preaching is a great and honorable calling. It is a noble ambition and a rescue mission rolled into one. Preaching is a mandate and a lifestyle. It is the highest of callings! The God of heaven and earth chose you! He anointed you and He has sent you. Now, there is only one thing to do: go forth and preach!

Preach with power. Preach with authority. Preach with conviction and reality. Preach as an ambassador of your office. For the prophet, teach and preach with insight and revelation. For the apostle, preach and teach the mystery that has been entrusted to you. Build and govern by the words of your mouth. Pastors, feed the flock! Establish the heart and mind of God in the midst of the sheep. For the evangelist, preach and demonstrate the good news of the Gospel. For the teacher, renew the mind of the corporate body of Christ. Challenge us, convict us, and equip us.

Dear friends, there are souls to save, nations to awaken, and a generation to reach. I say long live the preacher! Preach it strong, preach it loud, preach it boldly. Preach in the mountains and the valleys. Preach both in the good times and the bad. Preach with everything you've got. Let the message of Jesus go forth. The world needs the preacher.

## MY PRAYER FOR YOU

Father, in a day of trouble and calamity, I thank you for your chosen vessel. I pray that you fill their mouth with your word. I pray that you send them forth with both fire and authority. I break and bind the spirit of heaviness and command it to go. I thank you that this preacher knows you as Abba and speaks from a place of sonship and surrender. I thank you for revealing both your heart and mind to this preacher. I pray that you revive the preacher. Send the preacher. Anoint the preacher with fresh oil and power. Establish them in the earth for such a time as this. I thank you for their unique gift and view. I thank you that they effectively communicate all that you have placed inside of them. I pray for the spirit of wisdom and revelation to flow with ease into their life and ministry. I ask you to heal every wound and bind up all brokenness. I ask you to send them to the people you have appointed them to reach. I thank you for the reviving of their spirit today, in the name of Jesus. I thank you for the strong and bold call to preach. I pray for the right doors to open and the wrong ones to slam shut. I pray for a fresh wind to blow on their life and ministry. I pray for them to have prophetic encounters with you that blow their mind. I pray for the fiery coal to touch their lips. I pray for new levels of decree. I pray for new levels of wisdom. I pray for your words to flow from their lips like honey. I thank you for daring exploits in their life and ministry. I call this preacher blessed, and release your goodness in every area of their life and ministry, in the matchless name of Jesus. Amen!

**LONG LIVE THE PREACHER!**